Deserts

Ewan McLeish

Wayland

Our Green World

Acid Rain
Atmosphere
Deserts
Farming
Oceans
Polar Regions
Rainforests
Recycling
Wildlife

Cover: A gemsbok in the Namib Desert, in south-west Africa.

Book editor: Jannet King
Series editor: Philippa Smith
Series designer: Malcolm Walker

First published in 1992 by
Wayland (Publishers) Ltd
61 Western Road, Hove
East Sussex BN3 1JD, England

British Library Cataloguing in Publication Data
McLeish, Ewan
Deserts. – (Our green world)
I. Title II. Series
333.73

HARDBACK ISBN 0-7502-0303-X

PAPERBACK ISBN 0-7502-0861-9

Typeset by Kudos Editorial and Design Services, Sussex, England
Printed in Italy by G. Canale & C.S.p.A., Turin

Contents

Words printed in **bold** in the main text are explained in the glossary on page 45.

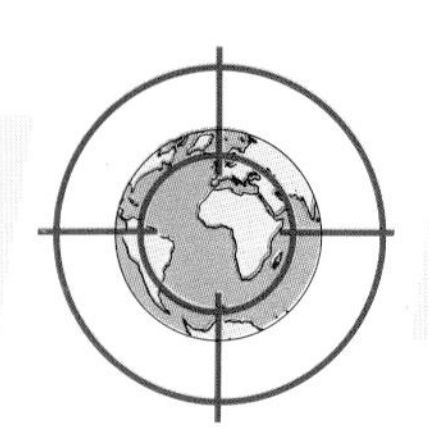

Introduction: two stories

The desert appears to be dead. There is no water, no life. Suddenly, the sky darkens. A flash of lightning splits the sky. The rain comes.

In ten minutes it is over. It may not rain again for another year. But something is stirring. The surface of the earth cracks and hundreds of toads climb out. They find shallow pools left by the rain and lay their eggs. Before the pools dry up the eggs must form tadpoles which grow into young toads. These toads then burrow into the mud to wait for the rains to return.

▼ *Storm clouds gather over the lifeless desert.*

▲ *After the rain the desert comes to life.*

▲ *Toads crawl out of the earth and lay eggs.*

◀ *These eggs develop into tadpoles.*

▲ *Goats eat the trees and trample any grass which has managed to grow. The thin, dry soil is blown away.*

Talah is nine years old. She used to live with her family in a small village in West Africa. But their land was taken by a company that wanted to grow cotton on it. The family were forced to move their farm to land where the soil was poor. For two years it did not rain, so the crops Talah and her family had planted died. Goats trampled the soil and trees were cut down for firewood. Nothing was left.

Carrying their belongings, they walked many kilometres to a camp where food was being brought by truck.

Talah and her family still live in the camp. They cannot return to their village because the land has been turned into a desert by people and their animals. It is not a natural, living desert like the one in the first story, but an unnatural, dead area which is spreading year by year.

Women and children wait for water in a camp in Africa. ▶

▼ *The villages which they were forced to leave are now part of the desert.*

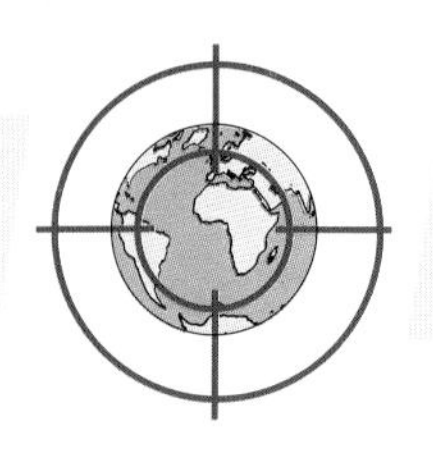

The living desert

You can see from the map that deserts are found all around the world. They occur where the sun is very hot and winds are dry.

Some deserts are made up of kilometres of sand, but others are just bare rock and gravel.

The largest desert in the world is the Sahara. It is 5000 km across — nearly as wide as the Atlantic Ocean. ▶

▲ *This building in Australia is being buried by drifting sand.*

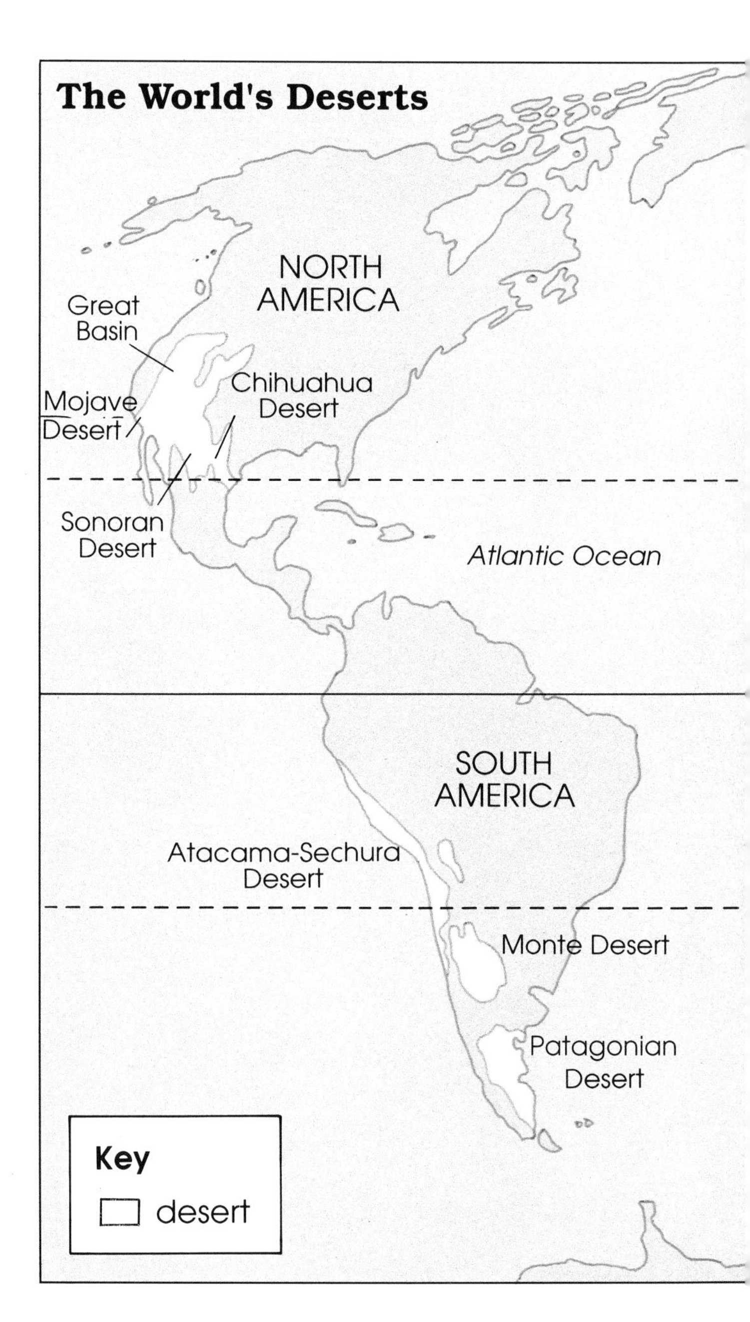

Deserts can get very hot, especially in summer. But at night they quickly cool down and may even freeze. It may rain only once a year. ▶

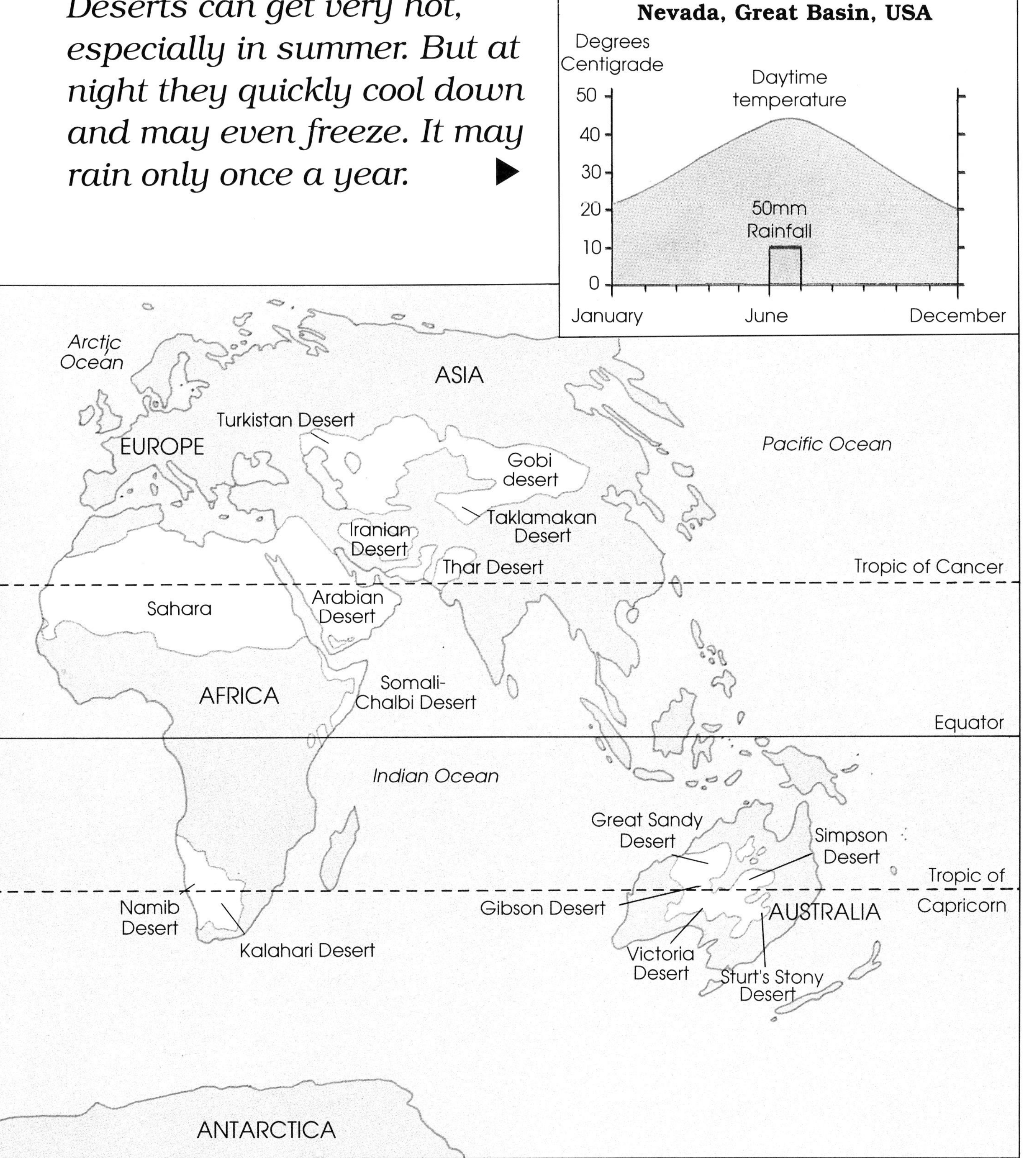

▲ *Deserts occur where the wind has passed over thousands of kilomertes of land, or over mountain ranges, losing all its moisture on the way.*

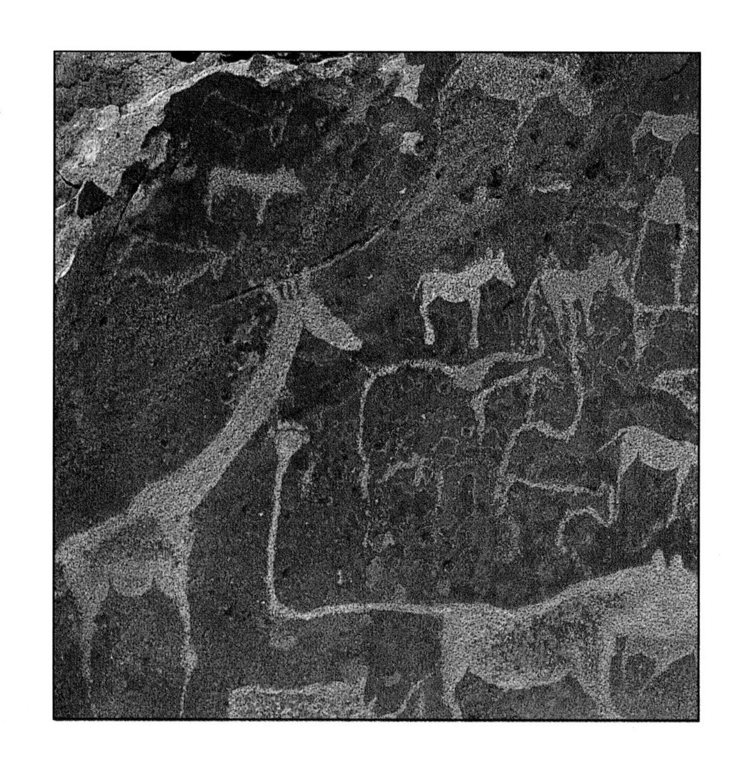

These paintings, found in a cave in an African desert, show us that this was once a ***fertile*** *land. Changes in the climate have made it a desert.* ▶

▼ *This squirrel uses its tail as a sunshade. The scorpion below has a hard shell which stops it losing too much water.*

▼ *These plants are good at soaking up and storing water.*

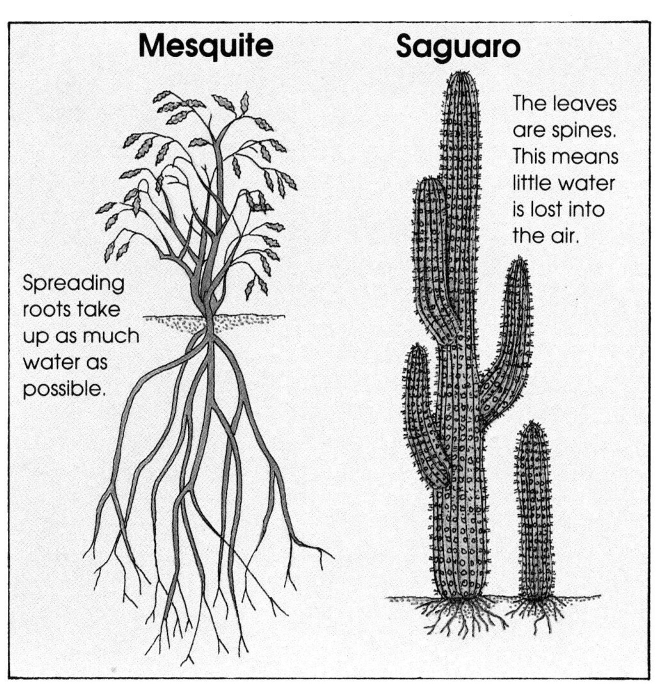

▼ *Namibian sand grouse soak their feathers in water and carry it back to their young.*

▲ *The fennec fox has huge ears. They allow heat to escape from the fox's body and help to keep it cool.*

Many of the animals that live in the desert stay under shady rocks for most of the day. They come out to hunt for food in the evening, when the air is cooler.

Cold-blooded animals like lizards, snakes and scorpions need the warmth of their surroundings to keep them moving. As the night gets colder they begin to slow down and return to their **crevices**. Even warm-blooded animals, such as foxes and mice, soon find it too cold and go back to their dens.

▼ *The Gila monster from the American West comes out to hunt in the early morning. Before long it is forced by the heat to look for shelter.*

Not only animals live in deserts – people live there too. Imagine one of them now walking slowly across the desert, looking for water. He finds an old, dried-up plant and digs until he finds its root. It is the size of a football. He pulls it up, grates it with a knife and squeezes it between his hands. A trickle of liquid appears and he drinks. There is no other water anywhere.

▼ *This is the Australian outback. Could you survive here?*

▲ *Australian bushmen survive because they understand their surroundings. This strangely-shaped rock makes the smallest noise sound loud.*

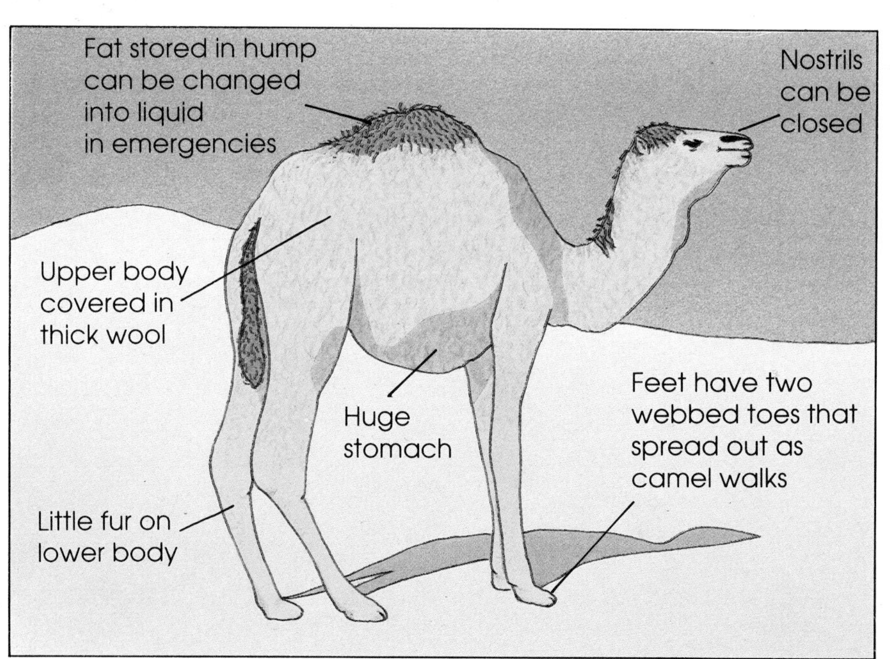

▲ *A* ***caravan*** *of Tuareg nomads crossing the Sahara.*

◀ *The camel has ways of surviving in the desert.*

An oasis. ▶

Some people who live in the desert use camels to travel long distances. The Tuareg are **nomads**. They cross from the north of the Sahara Desert, with gold, dates and silk, to trade with the people of the south. But they could not travel across the desert without oases. At an oasis, water comes close to the surface of the land. Oases form little islands of green in the sea of sand and rock.

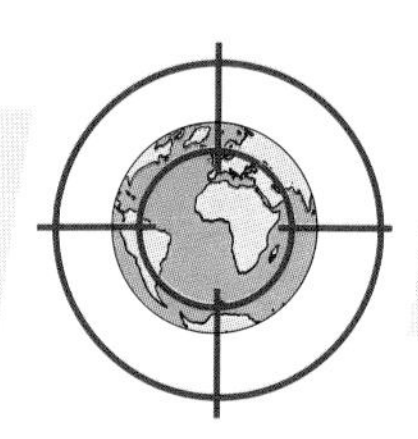

The desert spreads

▲ *Have you noticed what happens when people and animals take a short cut across the grass? The grass is worn away and a dusty path appears.* ▲

Have you ever been out for a walk after heavy rain and seen mud or gravel washed onto the road? Have you ever heard the wind whistling down the street, and felt the dust stinging your face?

If you have, then you already know something about how deserts spread. Now we will see why.

The Great Plains of the American Midwest were once fertile farm lands. But as more and more of the Plains were ploughed up to grow wheat, the land was damaged. In 1930 and 1931, two years of **drought** were followed by great storms. The wind blew 350 million tonnes of dry soil away, blacking out the sun. The area became known as the Great Dustbowl. A large part of America had become a desert.

Can you see that this story is like the earlier story about Talah? They are both about how people affect their surroundings and make deserts.

An American farming family leaves its ruined land in the 1930s. ▶

If deserts are natural, what is the problem? The real problem is not the deserts themselves, but the areas around them. These areas are still quite dry, but they are also fertile and therefore good for farming.

The problem comes if these areas are not used wisely.

▼ *This land is being well used. But it could become like the picture on page 14.*

▲ *People need to cut down trees for firewood. But if all the trees are taken then the soil may be blown or washed away.*

Soil **erosion** can occur if too many sheep are brought in to **graze** the grass, or if crops die because there is no rain.

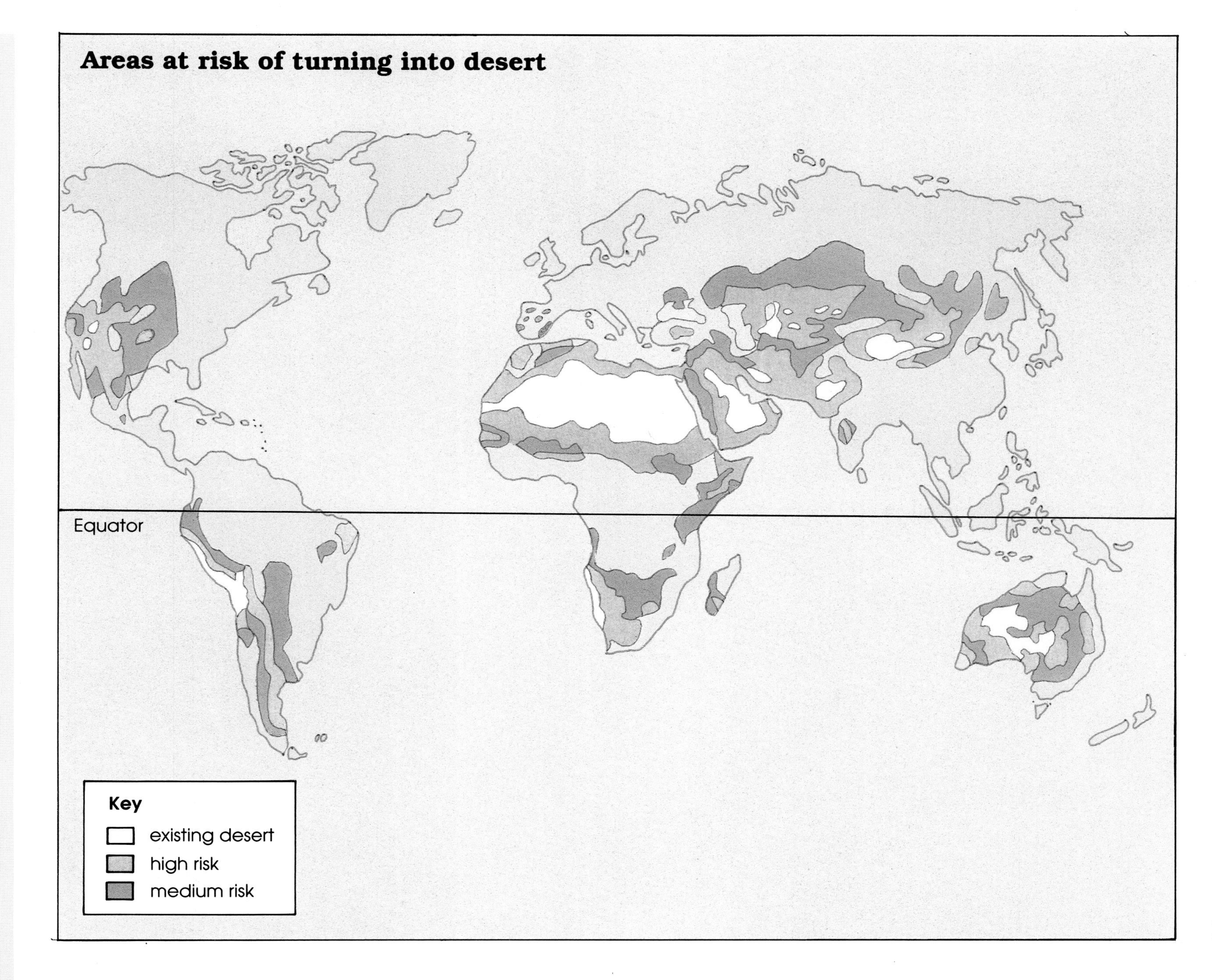

Areas at risk of turning into desert
Equator
Key
existing desert
high risk
medium risk

Look at the map on the opposite page. The areas shown in brown are those which are in most danger of turning into desert.

About 300 million people live in these areas. (That is more than all the people in the United States.)

▲ *Like Talah, in the story at the beginning of the book, these children have had to leave their homes. This is because their families can no longer grow crops on their land.*

Desert sand covers the street in this town in Chad, Africa. ▶

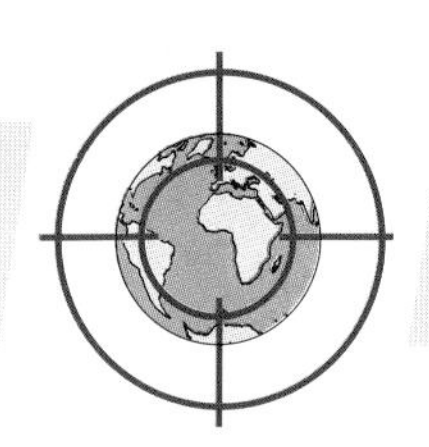

Why deserts spread

▲ *These women are pounding millet. This is a crop which grows well in dry areas.*

As we have seen, the dry areas around deserts are often very fertile. Here, people can live well from the crops they grow and the animals they keep. But the soil has to be used wisely. Every few years it must be left to lie **fallow**, or be used only for grazing. Then it can recover its goodness before being used again.

The number of people in the world is growing and more food is needed. Farmers no longer feel able to leave their land unused. They grow crops on it every year to feed their families. The trouble is that the soil becomes exhausted, so that less, rather than more, food is produced.

▼ *At this market in Morocco, animals are exchanged for grain or vegetables.*

There is another reason why deserts are created. It has to do with the fact that poor countries need to earn money by growing crops that rich countries will buy. These crops include tea, coffee, peanuts, cotton and chocolate. They are called cash crops.

The companies growing the cash crops may force farmers to leave their good land. They may have to move to land which is not so good. We saw what happened to Talah's family. The new land they tried to farm turned to desert.

Another cause of deserts is, strangely enough, water!

In order to grow better crops, water is brought in from somewhere else. This may be from deep wells, or by pumping or channelling water from a river.

If the land is not well drained, the soil becomes too wet. Salts in the water can poison the plants and the land becomes useless for growing crops. Then people leave the land and more deserts are formed.

▲ *This **irrigation** project in West Africa will greatly improve the **yield** of the crop. But such projects must be looked after carefully — otherwise they can do more harm than good.*

◀ *A cash crop being sprayed with chemicals to protect it from pests.*

In dry lands the nomadic herders try to keep their flocks of sheep and goats, and herds of cattle, on the move. They know where the good grazing is, and where the rain falls. They try to spread out their herds to avoid damaging the **fragile** land.

But as the number of people increases, the herds are also growing bigger. At the same time, more and more land is being cleared and ploughed up to plant more crops.

Farmers and herders used to help each other to manage the land properly. But now animals often trample and chew everything in sight.

This soil erosion in Kenya, East Africa, has been caused by ***over-grazing****. Now the rain is washing the soil away.* ▶

Deserts are not only growing in Africa. In the dry parts of the United States, Canada and Australia, cattle and sheep **ranching** are causing exactly the same problems. Deserts affect rich and poor countries alike.

▲ *This desert in Australia has been caused by over-grazing.*

Rangelands to wastelands

In the United States erosion of soil has halved the production of grass on many of the **rangelands** or ranches.

In Australia grazing rabbits, sheep and cattle, which have been brought from other countries, have caused the **extinction** of many kinds of plants and animals.

Wood is very useful. You can build houses with it, or cook and keep warm with it. Half the world depends on wood.

So half the world collects wood, usually as fallen branches, but also by cutting down whole trees. Sometimes, large areas of forest are cut down to clear land for growing crops. Trees provide food and shelter for animals. Tree roots hold the soil in place. Without trees, much land turns into desert.

Wood for fuel

These women may have to walk for four to six hours, three times a week, to gather wood to cook their evening meal. ▶

▲ *Wood for sale in West Africa. As wood becomes harder to find, its price rises and poor people cannot afford it.*

So who is to blame for the spread of deserts? We have learned that drought on its own does not cause deserts. People cause deserts, but in ways that are very complicated and which involve all of us.

If people can create deserts, it should be possible for them to stop deserts spreading too.

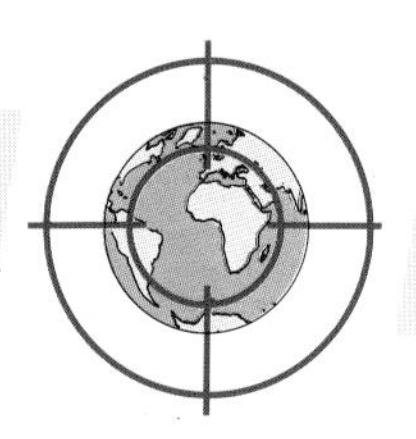

Turning back the deserts

Much is being done to try and halt the spread of deserts. People in the countries affected, and **aid workers** from other countries, are trying hard to solve the problem.

It is not always easy. Often money meant to help people like Talah and her family is used to build roads or cities instead. This may help those who live in cities, but not the people in the country who just want some fertile land to farm.

▲ *Animals crowd round water tanks provided by the government, eroding the soil with their hooves.*

▲ *Food aid arrives in the Sudan, Central Africa. But getting it to people who need it will be difficult.*

It is important for rich countries to send food to poor countries in **emergencies**. But this may create more problems. 'Free' food from the government and **aid agencies** lowers the price of food produced by local farmers. This makes it hard for farmers to survive.

Money is sent to help local farmers grow more food. But too often it is spent on cash crops instead, which are then sold abroad.

Money must be spent on helping people to help themselves.

We often hear poor countries being blamed for their large populations. But this chart shows that rich countries also have high **population densities**.

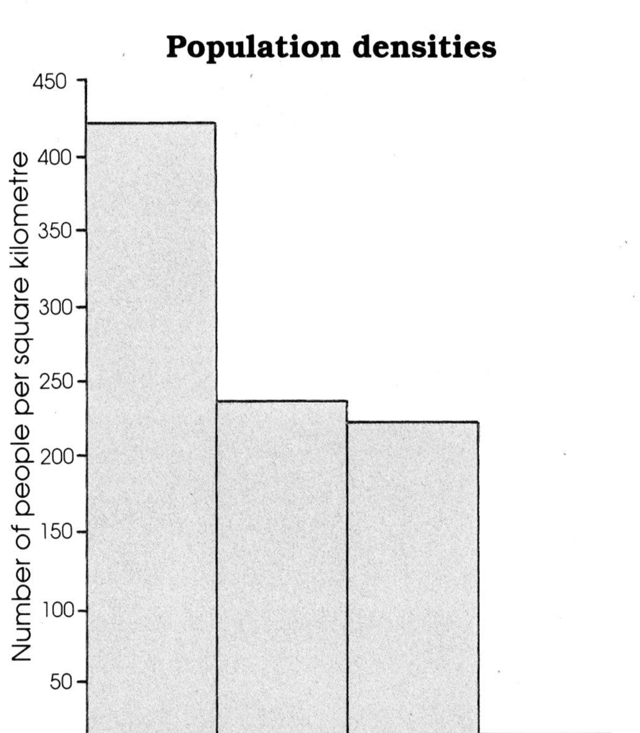

This chart shows how some African countries owe billions of dollars to Western countries. So they have no money to stop the spread of deserts.

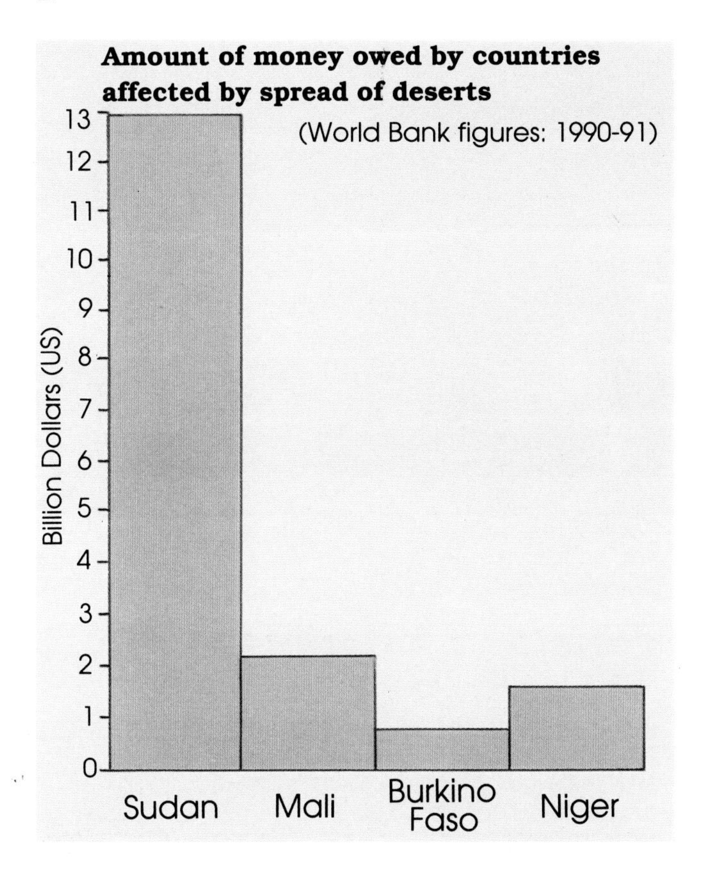

Rich countries like the USA use up more food than they can grow. And their desert problem is as serious as many poor countries.

We must change many things in order to stop the deserts spreading.

The diagram below shows some of the ways of stopping the spread of deserts (although they would not all be used in the same place, or at the same time).

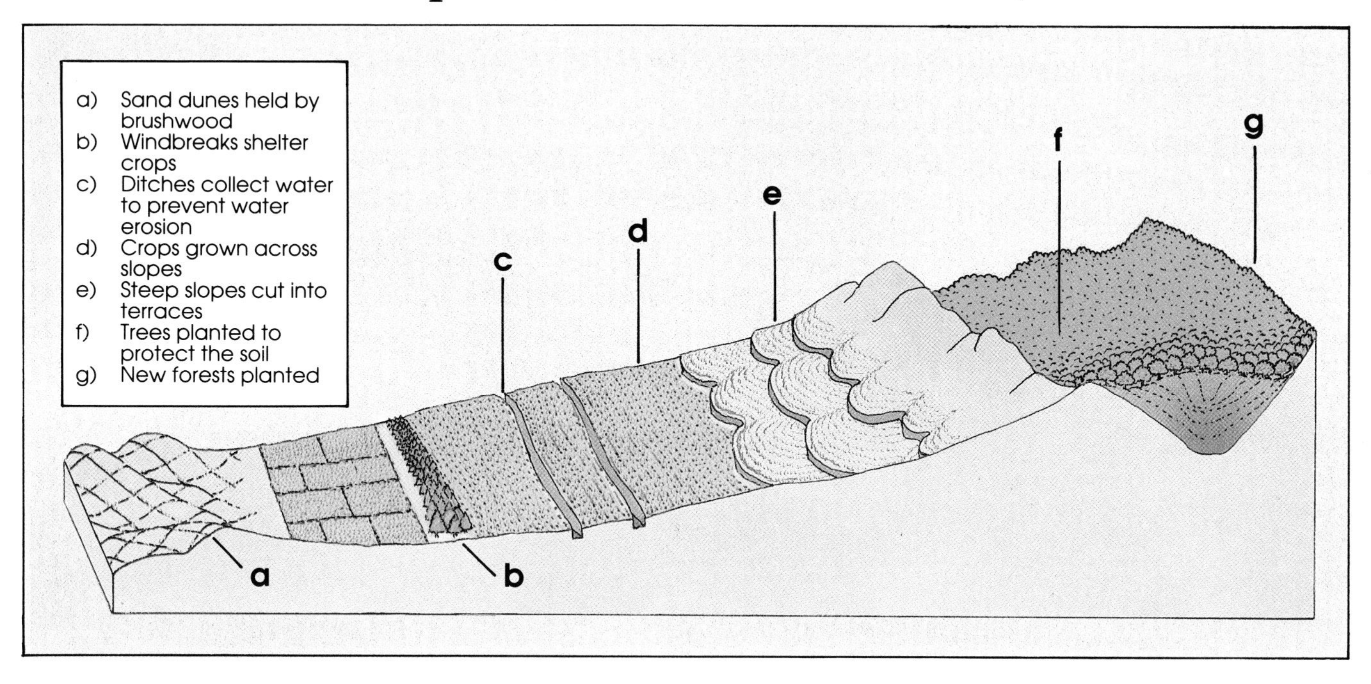

Working it out

Try this experiment to test whether it is better to farm across a slope or down it.

- Using corrugated plastic, make a slope with the ridges and furrows running up and down.
- Cover the plastic with a layer of sand. What happens when you pour water gently on the slope?
- Now make a slope with the ridges running across. Pour on the water again. What happens and what does it show?

The diagram above shows some of the answers which have been found in the fight against the spread of deserts. But the ways people use the land still have to change.

Getting the best out of crops

In order to grow more crops without damaging the soil, better farming methods are needed.

One way is to use **fertilizers**, but these may also damage the soil and are expensive. A better way is to grow different crops in different years. Then the goodness in the soil does not get used up.

Scientists are developing new **varieties** of crops that produce more grain, or will grow with very little water. And villagers can grow different kinds of food by planting orchards and vegetable gardens next to wells.

Better ways of storing grain must be found so that there is enough food even for bad years.

These crops are being tested to see if they will grow in drought conditions. ▶

Stopping over-grazing

One of the reasons why deserts form is that goats and cattle eat all the plants. Their hooves damage the soil, which is blown or washed away. Smaller herds, kept on the move, would cause less damage.

A healthy animal may produce twice as much milk as a sick one. But a healthy animal will not eat twice as much food. Smaller herds of healthy animals could produce as much milk as larger herds of unhealthy ones. So it is important to spend money on better care for animals.

But this might lead to bigger herds. Herdsmen may have to kill more cattle for meat, or trade with farmers and swop animals for grain. This will only work if the farmers have enough grain to trade. The spread of deserts can only be stopped if farmers and herdsmen work together.

▲ *This Addax can travel a long way without water.*

Cattle do not like walking a long way or going without water. If herdsmen had animals like the Addax antelope they would be able to travel further in search of food.

Bringing back the forests

▲ *Only 20 years ago this land was covered in trees.*

Do you remember where Talah lived? If trees go on being cut down in her country at the present rate, in 20 years time there will be no woodland left.

So the answer is to plant more trees and to protect those that are already there.

Crops can be grown underneath certain types of tree, like the acacia. The roots of the acacia tree make the soil richer, and its seed pods can be fed to the animals.

Shelter belts

All over the world, shelter belts, made of rows of of trees or cactuses, are being planted to protect crops from the wind. Often the trees can be harvested for animal food and firewood.

▲ *Cactus in Nigeria, West Africa, planted as a windbreak.*

▲ *These women are using branches to form windbreaks.*

Getting people together

Villages in India work together to plant trees on common land. They plant different types of trees that they can use for different things: firewood, animal feed and building.

The villagers protect the trees from grazing animals and from people who might steal the wood. They share the wood and the money made from selling it.

▲ *An aid worker gives advice to a villager.*

So what have we found out about the spread of deserts?

We know that deserts are not just caused by drought or bad luck or by too many people. They are caused by **poverty**, by the bad use of land, and by the way countries treat one another.

We also know that people working together, and understanding what they are doing, can stop the spread of deserts.
The nations of the world must now work together to do this.

▲ *This new forest, planted in North Africa, is beginning to turn back the desert.*

◀ ***Terraces** built on this hill in Ethiopia, Africa, help prevent soil erosion.*

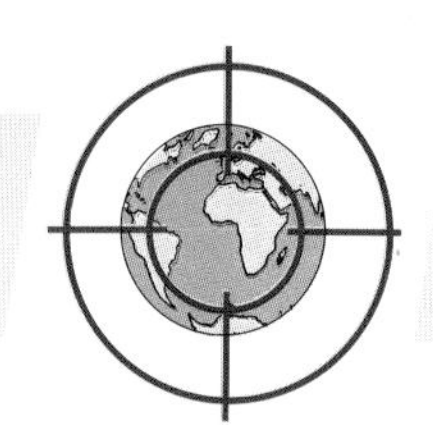

But what can I do?

This soil erosion has happened in the Peak District, one of Britain's national parks. What do you think has caused it? ▶

You can probably see now that almost all countries have a problem of soil erosion, which leads to deserts. And you also know that problems (and answers) don't just stop at the edge of one country. So it is not just somebody else's problem; it is ours too.

Here are some ideas about how you can help:

- When you are out walking, keep to footpaths and don't walk more than two abreast.
- Look for examples of erosion where you live or go to school. How could it be stopped?
- Join an **environmental group** which fights against deserts spreading. Or join a local group that helps to protect your own surroundings.

- Look out for news in papers and magazines about the spread of deserts in your own country and abroad. Tell other people about it!

- Look at pages 26 and 27 again. Think about how the things you see around you affect the spread of deserts.

▲ *This cash crop is sugar cane. It earns money for a poor country, but the land may be damaged.*

▲ *This was once fertile land. Now it is desert. We can all help to stop this happening again.*

Glossary

Aid agencies Organizations that help poor countries by providing emergency food, equipment, and education.

Aid worker Someone working for an aid agency.

Caravan A nomadic (travelling) group of people, usually carrying goods (for trading) on camels.

Crevices Cracks in rocks in which small animals can find shelter.

Drought A long period without rain.

Emergency A sudden crisis or danger, often to do with floods, drought or other disaster.

Environmental group A group of people that work together to try and protect our surroundings.

Erosion The wearing away of soil by wind or water, often after the loss of trees or grass due to over-grazing.

Extinction The loss of a particular plant or animal, often by the action of people.

Fallow Leaving a piece of land uncultivated (unfarmed) for a period of time to allow the soil to recover its goodness.

Fertile Used to describe soil rich in nutrients (goodness), and good for growing crops.

Fertilizer A chemical or animal product added to soil to make it more fertile.

Fragile Easily damaged.

Graze To feed on grass.

Irrigation Ways of bringing water to dry areas, such as with wells, pumps or canals.

Nomads Travelling people who take all their belongings, including animals, with them.

Over-grazing This occurs when too many animals (sheep, goats or cattle) are allowed to feed in one place.

Population density A measure of how crowded a country is, usually given as the number of people per square kilometre.

Poverty Lack of money.

Ranching Raising of cattle or sheep on large areas of land.

Rangelands Large areas of grassed land, usually used for raising cattle.

Terraces Sloping land cut into steps to make level areas for growing crops.

Varieties Different types of a particular plant or crop which have different qualities, for example, the ability to grow in dry conditions, or to resist disease.

Yield The amount of grain or other food a particular crop can produce.

Finding out more

Books to read

The Desert by Lionel Bender (Franklin Watts, 1989)
Deserts by Tom Mariner (Cherrytree, 1988)
In a Desert by Barrie Watts (Franklin Watts, 1991)
Life in the Deserts by Lucy Baker (Two-Can, 1990)
Wild World of Animals: Deserts by Michael Chinery (Kingfisher, 1991)

Useful addresses

Australian Association for
 Environmental Education
GPO Box 12
Canberra
ACT 2601

Council for Environmental
 Education
University of Reading
London Road
Reading RG1 5AQ

Friends of the Earth (Australia)
National Liaison Office
366 Smith Street
Collingwood
Victoria 3065

Friends of the Earth (Canada)
Suite 53
54 Queen Street
Ottawa KP5 C5

Friends of the Earth
 (New Zealand)
Nagal House
Courthouse Lane
PO Box 39/065
Auckland West

Friends of the Earth (UK)
26-28 Underwood Street
London N1 7JC

Oxfam (UK)
274 Banbury Road
Oxford OX2 7DZ

United Nations Environment
 Programme (UK)
c/o IIED
3 Endsleigh Street
London WC1H 0DD

WATCH
The Green
Witham Park
Lincoln LN5 7JR

World Wide Fund for Nature
 (UK)
Panda House
Weyside Park
Godalming
Surrey GU7 1QU

Index

Picture acknowledgements
Bruce Coleman Ltd 4 (Paul Wakefield), 5 (top/B & C Calhoun), 5 (below right/J Cancalosi), 8 (John R Brownlie), 11 (below right/Jen & Des Bartlett), 12 (Sullivan & Rogers), 13 (Steve Kaufman), 16 (Henneghien), 17 (Ken Lambert), 18 (left/L C Marigo), 24 (B & C Alexander), 28 (Peter Davey), 29 (David Austen), 37 (Erwin & Peggy Bauer); Hutchison Library 6, 7, 23, 25, 30, 36 (right), 41 (below); Frank Lane Picture Agency 11 (top and below left), 18 (right), 42; Peter Newark's Western Americana 19; Christine Osborne Pictures 20, 26, 32, 41 (top), Oxfam Picture Library 21, 23, 33, 38, 39, 40 (all by Jeremy Hartley), 31 (Nick Haslam), 39 (Anna Tulley), 43 (F Rubin); Oxford Scientific Films *cover* (Anthony Bannister), 5 (below right/Rodger Jackman), 14 (David Curl), 36 (centre/Jack Dermid), ZEFA 44, 15 (Robin Smith). All artwork is by Marilyn Clay.